A Little Book

From Stressed to Blessed

5 Simple Steps
to Learn Meditation
and Change Your Life

Cynthia D. Chase
MA, CHTHA

Cover Design by Christos Angelidakis

ISBN-978-0-578-77254-7

Dedication

To all of my beloved children

Tyler, Kyle, David, Cooper, and Cassie. Your presence has been a joy in my life. When I think of you, my heart fills with love. I appreciate how we (all twenty of us!) have fun adventures, share our stories, and support each other. May you and your families always remember, "I love you THIS MUCH!"

To my beloved husband Robert

You are the other half that makes me whole. Your caring, kind, supportive ways have strengthened me and all our family. You are loved and respected not only by our tribe but by all who know you. Thank you for sharing your life with me and for your love that continues to grow my soul.

You have a treasure within you that is infinitely greater than anything the world can offer.

—Eckhart Tolle

Contents

Preface

I have written the following words on meditation for the sole purpose of guiding you from feeling "stressed to blessed" in your life.

May the time you spend in meditation be a wellspring of information and blessings, healing you from the inside out. May your blessings bring peace, love, and joy into your life and the lives of others, ultimately helping to positively change the world by bringing the same peace, love, and joy into the world at large.

—*Cynthia D. Chase*

From Stressed to Blessed

Are you stressed?

There are many reasons why we feel stress in life. Family problems, ill health, financial problems, addiction, divorce, the death of someone close to us, a stressful job or loss of a job, problems in school, or problems with relationships are just a few examples. The list could go on and on.

Wouldn't you like to improve your life by bringing in a greater sense of well-being, more meaning, and better health along with more happiness and joy, and a sense of gratitude for things in your life you previously didn't appreciate? Would you like to experience more peace, more inspiration, more energy, and vibrancy?

You will experience these positive benefits once you are on the path of practicing meditation. You will feel blessed!

When you make the present moment the focal point of your life instead of past or future, your ability to enjoy what you do-and with it, the quality of your life-increases dramatically.

—Eckhart Tolle

My Story

At the age of 36, I was separated from my then-husband, and I was a single mother of four children: a 1-year-old daughter, and three sons, ages 7, 8, and 10. Additionally, I was a graduate student pursuing a master's degree in counseling psychology with emphasis in depth psychology. I traveled from Northern California to Southern California once a month for two years for three days of classes, and I traveled abroad for two intense summer sessions. The amount of course work was monumental. My thoughts: "How am I going to handle all of this?"

I soon realized I would be better able to cope with the situation by practicing meditation and reconnecting to my spirituality that was firmly rooted in my early childhood.

Meditation is not a way of making your mind quiet, it's a way of entering into the quiet that's already there buried under 50,000 thoughts the average person thinks every day.

—Deepak Chopra

One of my first childhood memories goes back to the time when I was 4 years old. I was walking up the many well-worn white steps of a big red building that was home to the Methodist church in Hendersonville, North Carolina. I felt secure as my small left hand was gently held in my father's large, strong right hand.

As we stepped through the wide double doors into the foyer of the church, I remember feeling the presence of something that was much greater than I was.

Know there is something bigger than you guiding you, embracing you, and taking care of you.

—Anita Moorjani

Throughout my childhood, I was fortunate to have had this comforting presence in my life. In the years to follow, my life was busy with many demands and responsibilities I faced as an adult, which included working three jobs during one period of time. There were many wonderful, joyful experiences along the way, and there were tearful, sad experiences as well. I learned that when I was able to consciously focus on the awareness and connection with the Divine, with God (I refer to Divine energy as God), circumstances always shifted and ultimately for the better!

Meditation is how I focused on the awareness of and connection with Spirit. The time I spent in silence in prayer and meditation opened my eyes and my heart to new awareness and knowings about life.

I was introduced to meditation by a friend while attending graduate school. I was a mid-life, career-change adult. Meditation changed my life.

Meditation was explained to me by another meditation class participant as: "Prayer is the time you talk with God. Meditation is the time God talks with you."

We are here to find the dimension within ourselves that is deeper than thought.

—Eckhart Tolle

My meditation teacher was a fabulous, extremely knowledgeable, well-traveled, and kind gentleman by the name of Robert Ayres. Robert came into my life when I was in great need of guidance, which he provided by teaching me meditation. After practicing two times, I was hooked. I found meditation to be a calming force in the midst of all that I was experiencing. During a class one evening, Robert taught the class how the benefits of meditation could be experienced on a soul-level. This teaching has always stayed with me. To paraphrase Robert:

For someone who has had a meditation practice for a period of time, the effect of trauma on the soul-level is as though you are able to write in the sky with your finger. It is effortless and leaves no trace.

For someone who has experienced meditation a handful of times, the effect of trauma on the soul-level could be akin to using a stick to write in sand. The effect of trauma is semi-permanent.

For someone who experiences trauma in life, and they have never experienced meditation, the effect on the soul-level could be likened to using a sharp stick to etch into the hard surface of a rock. The effect of trauma is permanent.

An experience I had several years ago will illustrate how meditation can be a positive force in your life:

Life was super busy as I tried to stay in touch with our large immediate family (nineteen of us) living in various locations. I was up at 4:45 AM every day but Sunday, worked until almost midnight most nights trying to stay on top of my work, and I was one day into a "leave caffeine behind" plan.

I was driving home midday on a Saturday in August after working double-time at a church where I volunteered to help the homeless and people in need. After a visit to the grocery store for some special treats for one of our sons and his family who were coming to visit, I fell asleep driving down my street. My car went off the road, through a neighbor's wire fence, hit a tree, and stopped within inches of a ravine. When the impact occurred, I was jolted awake as the airbags inflated.

Smoke was streaming up out of my steering wheel, and the air was pungent. I knew I needed to quickly exit the car. As I opened my door and stepped out, I looked down into a steep ravine inches from where my tires came to rest. I checked to see if I had any injuries, which, thankfully, I did not, and then took my pocketbook and a couple of my belongings out of my car. The peach pie that was to have been dessert that night was splattered around the car like modern art!

I did not panic. I did not cry. I was calm. My lucid state and absence of panic were the result of my time in meditation over the years. This was a perfect example of Robert's teaching.

A visit to the doctor was necessary because my chest and shins were a little sore and I needed clearance to attend a retreat in Sedona the next week. The doctor gave me the go-ahead but followed by saying, "Most people who have the airbag deploy end up with broken ribs and shins." In other words, I was lucky. I knew I was blessed. At the time of the accident, I had felt my dad's presence and Divine energy surrounding me and protecting me until my husband arrived.

I used my husband's car to drive into town the following day. I experienced no anxiety as I passed the site of the accident—it was like writing in the sky with my finger.

I am convinced that having meditated throughout the years enabled me to stay calm and centered during a stressful, frightening, and dangerous situation. A quiet mind is better able to hear the soft, reassuring voice of Spirit.

Calmness of mind is one of the beautiful jewels of wisdom.

—James Allen

Five Simple Steps To Meditation

The more regularly and the more deeply you meditate, the sooner you will find yourself acting from a center of peace.

—Eckhart Tolle

Step 1
Where to Meditate

Finding a comfortable space and place is crucial to a positive meditation experience. Find an area in your home where you feel at ease and you have privacy. The most important key to have a successful meditation is to find a QUIET place. You will find that being jolted awake when you are in a meditative state is an extremely jarring experience that, as Robert taught, can upturn your meditation and leave you feeling agitated for the rest of the day. I have experienced this. It is true.

Please turn off your phone. If you have pets that lick, snore, or make any kind of noise, it is best to lovingly put them outside your space for the time you are meditating. If you have children, the same applies. Try to meditate at a time they will not disturb you.

If they are old enough to understand, try to explain the importance of their being quiet while you have this time to yourself. It only takes a handful of meditation sessions and your family members and those close to you will notice the calm and more aware presence you have attained.

Learn to be calm and you will always be happy.

—Paramanhasa Yogananda

Step 2
Sitting Position

Find a comfortable chair, a thick cushion on the floor, the side of your bed, a bench, or whatever is in your private space for sitting. Lying on your back on the floor, a bed, or outside on the ground is also a position for meditating. The aim is to have a straight spine, whether sitting up or lying down. If you fall asleep more than a couple of times, you may want to think about sitting.

As for the position of your hands, choose a position that is most comfortable for you. If you are sitting, try placing your hands with palms facing up on the top of your legs. Or you may prefer placing your left hand in the palm of your right hand with your thumb tips touching, forming a circle. If you are lying down, place your arms by your side or spread a little wider distance from your body with your palms up. The position you are most comfortable with is the best for your meditation.

Feelings come and go like clouds in the sky. Conscious breathing is my anchor.

—Thich Nhat Hahn

Step 3
Breathing Method

Gently close your eyes and slowly inhale through your nose to the count of four, hold the breath to the count of four, gently exhale through your nose to the count of four, and hold to the count of four.

Continue this breathing pattern to the count of four for five minutes: gently inhale, hold the breath, gently exhale, hold, inhale, hold the breath, exhale, hold.

Your mind and body will begin to more fully relax with each breath, and this is best for a good meditation.

Meditation is the discovery that the point of life is always arrived at in the immediate moment.

—Alan Watts

Step 4
Begin to Meditate

Meditation works by allowing the calmness in your mind created by the breathing exercise to come forth. Gently close your eyes, relax, be comfortable, and have no expectations. Just allow the experience to unfold.

All meditators have intrusive thoughts, more so as you are learning to meditate, but there are ways to work with thoughts, so your mind remains calm and aware. Here are some ways to deal with these thoughts:

1) The thought arises, "Oh no! I forgot to call Dad back." Say to yourself, "That's OK, after I meditate I'll tend to that."

2) Prepare a table in your mind's eye, and when a thought comes, gently place it there.

3) In your mind's eye, place your thoughts into flowing river water.

4) Place your thought inside a balloon, and watch as it rises up into the sky.

5) When a thought comes into your mind, gently notice the open space between the words of the thought, then keep your attention there as long as possible.

6) Place your attention on the middle of your forehead, slightly above the spot between your eyebrows when a thought arises.

7) When a thought comes, silently and slowly use a mantra to ease the thought away. A mantra is a word or words that, when repeated, help you to focus during meditation. Here are some possible mantras:

- I am love.

- Love is good.

- *Om Shanti, Shanti, Shanti.* [Peace, Peace, Peace.]

- *So Hum.* [I am.]

You will notice a calming of your thoughts as you choose the suggestion that works best for you.

Meditate for 20 minutes at each sitting if possible. After a handful of meditations, you will notice your mind begins to gently come back into the present moment in just that amount of time.

Meditate twice a day as close to the same times as possible; for example, in the morning just after awakening and in the late afternoon or early evening. This will help to support and strengthen a successful practice.

If your schedule has limited time for meditating, consider sitting for 5, 10, or 15 minutes. Some time is better than none!

You will appreciate the changes in your mind, body, and spirit as you engage these tips.

Real meditation has no direction or goal. It is pure wordless surrender, pure silent prayer.

—Adyashanti

Step 5
Coming Back to the Present

As you begin coming out of the meditation, take a few moments and notice your breath and the energy flowing through your body. Slowly open your eyes. Remain silent as long as possible, so you can fully appreciate the benefits of your meditation.

Journaling pages are included in the back of the book. As you are sitting in silence, review what your meditation experience was like. Were you able to experience moments of silence? Did a thought, phrase, or emotion come into your mind that was significant for you? Any pictures or colors? Write or draw what came up for you during your meditation.

Words and images sometimes give us messages that help us better understand our lives.

A Brief History of Meditation

Wall art in India depicting meditation has been dated as far back as circa 5000 BCE. Over time, the practice of meditation spread into neighboring areas and was modified and incorporated into a number of Eastern religions including Hinduism, Taoism, and Buddhism.[1]

Around the time of the American Revolution (1765), meditation began to spread in the West, spurred on by increased communication between cultures around the world.[2]

In 1893, Chicago, Illinois held the World Parliament of Religions. The event resulted in the increased awareness of meditation in

[1] Giovanni (15 August). "The History of Meditation (A 5,000 Years Timeline) Live and Dare." Retrieved 10 November 2019.
[2] Gustave Reininger, ed. (1997). "Centering Prayer in Daily Life and Ministry," New York: Continuum.

the Western world as Eastern teachings were shared by their spiritual teachers.[3]

A surge in the practice of meditation has continued to the present time.

---

[3] Eugene Taylor (1999). Michael Murphey; Steve Donovan: Eugene Taylor (eds.). Introduction: The Physical and Psychological Effects of Meditation: A Review of Contemporary Research With a Comprehensive Bibliography, 193.

From the Author

From Stressed to Blessed is loosely based on the style of meditation I first learned, transcendental meditation, or TM. Other meditation styles from retreats, lectures, and workshops I attended over time also have had some influence on my practice and the "5 Simple Steps to Learning Meditation" that I share.

I wrote this book as a very simple guide to help you get started with a meditation practice. As you meditate on a consistent basis, you will reach deeper states of awareness and experience a more enlightened life.

I am sending love and best wishes to you for a successful and fulfilling meditation practice.

Namaha—the Divine in me honors the Divine in you and all others.

—Cynthia Chase

Famous Quotes

May the words of my mouth and the meditation of my heart be pleasing to you, O Lord, my rock and redeemer.

—Psalm 19:14

The mind is definitely something that can be transformed and meditation is a means to transform it.

—14th Dalai Lama

Awareness is the greatest agent for change.

—Eckhart Tolle

Once you believe in yourself and see your soul as Divine and Precious, you'll automatically be converted to a being who can create miracles.

—Dr. Wayne Dyer

The quieter you become, the more you can hear.

—Baba Ram Das

Brilliant things happen in calm minds. Be calm. You're brilliant.

—@Headspace #mindfulmoments

Be the peace you want to see in the world.

—Gandhi

The treasure of unity is found by those who look within.

—Rumi

One evening as Isaac was walking and meditating in the fields, he looked up and saw the camels coming.

—Genesis 24–6 3

There is always a reason to be grateful.

—Deepak Chopra

Stillness is where creativity and solutions are found.

—Eckhart Toll

Quiet the mind and the soul will speak.

—Ma Jaya Sati Bhagavati

Where there is peace and meditation, there is no anxiety or doubt.

—Sir Francis de Sales

When you change the way you look at things, the things you look at change.

—Dr. Wayne Dyer

The presence of the living God is everywhere you go, all the time, every day.

—Steven Sadlier

Do not dwell in the past, do not dwell in the future, concentrate the mind on the present moment.

—Buddha

The secret to finding the deeper level in another is finding the deeper level in yourself. Without finding it in yourself, you cannot see it in the other.

—Eckhart Tolle

You shall meditate for 20 minutes a day unless you're too busy. Then you shall sit for an hour.

—Old Zen saying

Acknowledgments

Thank you to Robert Ayres for sharing your immense knowledge of meditation for the benefit of others. Your teachings have been a positive influence in my life, informing how I look at life and the world around me with new eyes and in a more enlightened way.

Thank you to my daughter, Cassie Anne, for the MANY hours you spent tutoring me and encouraging me about technological "stuff." I could not have completed this work without you.

And to my husband, Robert, thank you for sharing in life as the incredible partner you are. Thank you for supporting me as you overlooked piles of papers, late nights, questionable dinners, and thank you for helping with the self-editing of this book. You are the perfect example of "patience is a virtue."

Thank you to my friends, Marilyn O'Brien and Heidi Pace, for holding two-thirds of the sacred space we have shared from our days at Pacifica, to Greece, to Hawaii, and all the years that have followed. Your friendship and support have added a richness to life that will always stay with me.

To my friend and "little sister," Leah Guy, thank you for sharing and showing me how the sky is the limit, and there is always a way when it comes to setting and attaining goals in life. I cherish our many years of friendship and all we have shared.

Thank you to my "18 minute" friend, Alix Schmidt, for your support of my brochure, I mean booklet, I mean BOOK, and for your words of encouragement while I was writing. Your positive outlook uplifts many people, including me.

To my friends, Katy Biller, Susie Langeland, and Candy Wall, thank you for your years of friendship, support, and laughter, and for helping me see the goodness this book would bring people despite the hundred thousand books and videos out there.

About the Author

Cynthia Chase was born and raised in the majestic Blue Ridge Mountains of North Carolina. After graduating from the University of North Carolina-Chapel Hill with a degree in political science, she moved to North Lake Tahoe in California.

Cynthia holds a master's degree in counseling psychology with emphasis in depth psychology from Pacifica Graduate Institute in Santa Barbara, California. After obtaining a certification in clinical and medical hypnotherapy, she opened a practice in which she specialized working with surgical patients. Following her attendance at Michael Mamas' School for Healing and Enlightenment in San Diego, California, she expanded her work with clients to include a variety of healing practices.

In addition, Cynthia served as a ski minister on the slopes and a minister with the Wedding Chapel in North Lake Tahoe. She received her meditation teaching certificate from the Self Awareness Institute in Laguna Beach, California, and is a member of Celebrating Life Ministries.

Cynthia and her husband, Robert, live in the Gold Country of Northern California. They both delight in the joy of spending time with their five adult children and their spouses and significant others, and their eight precious grandkids.

Pages for Journaling

Made in the USA
Middletown, DE
10 April 2021

37343458R00047